100 WAYS TO HAPPY CHIC YOUR LIFE

Sterling Signature
NEW YORK

An Imprint of Sterling Publishing
387 Park Avenue South
New York, NY 10016

ISBN 978-1-4027-7507-9

Distributed in Canada by Sterling Publishing
c/o Canadian Manda Group, 165 Dufferin Street
Toronto, Ontario, Canada M6K 3H6
Distributed in the United Kingdom by GMC Distribution Services
Castle Place, 166 High Street, Lewes, East Sussex, England BN7 1XU
Distributed in Australia by Capricorn Link (Australia) Pty. Ltd.
P.O. Box 704, Windsor, NSW 2756, Australia

Design by ME&Friends LLC
Illustrations by Bruno Grizzo
Cover photo © Joshua McHugh
Jonathan Adler Executive Editor: Charlotte Hillman Warshaw

For information about custom editions, special sales, and premium and corporate purchases, please contact Sterling Special Sales at 800-805-5489 or specialsales@sterlingpublishing.com.

Manufactured in China

10 9 8 7 6 5 4 3 2 1

www.sterlingpublishing.com

JONATHAN ADLER
100
WAYS TO
HAPPY
CHIC
YOUR LIFE

Sterling Signature
NEW YORK

FOREWORD
BY DEBORAH NEEDLEMAN

INTRODUCTION

DWELL

EMBRACE

JONATHAN ADLER
KNOWS THE POINT OF A GREAT ROOM
IS NOT THE PEDIGREE

of the furniture or the color on the wall, but the creation of a warm, happy, welcoming space. Everything this brilliant man does is in the service of jolliness and good times, and for that, we—his fans—ought to be very grateful. Adler knows no one will go to their grave thinking, "If only I'd bought that Paul Evans console at auction or re-papered the living room with Scalamandré's zebra print." I, however, may go to my grave thinking about lovely times spent chez Adler.

Entering the Adler abode is a delirious feast for the senses, not simply because of the fabulous décor, but because the welcome is always squealy and excited, the guests sparkly and fun, the food delicious, the lighting flattering, and the chairs comfy. And of course, there are all the wonderful colors and patterns, and all the incredibly interesting *objets* to look at, every single place your eye might choose to land. Sitting on his fluffy rugs curled up next to someone in a cozy chair, with lovely scents wafting and happy chatter all around, is indeed the point of the whole decorating game. The stuff of a home is wonderful and worth our serious consideration. Searching for bits and bobs is enjoyable, rearranging it all is a pleasant compulsion, and staring lovingly at your nice things is indeed very nice. But really—and our Johnny knows this—making a home is *really* about making happiness. And there is no better guide on the quest to a more personable and personal home than Mr. Adler.

To think that not all that long ago, this man was simply redefining modern pottery with his cheeky chic striped vases and bowls. But then came his home accessories, followed by collections of furniture, followed by a career decorating houses and hotels, followed by lines of everything else imaginable, from bedding and towels to stationery and totes. Then, when there were no more décor categories left to re-imagine, he took on books, TV, and fashion, without ever losing a modicum of cuteness as his business grew ever more diverse and enviable. How was this possible, you ask? Because everything Jonathan Adler does is seamlessly in line with Jonathan Adler. His work is an authentic expression of his deliriously delightful personality. Jonathan Adler has chic'ed up our country, and now he has come to chic up your house. *I suggest you open your door, and let this nice man in.*

—DEBORAH NEEDLEMAN
Editor of *WSJ Magazine* & Founding Editor of *Domino*

There is no proper or correct way to decorate, just intriguing ways to DWELL in Happy Chic–ness…. There is no outfit that is too over the top…. There are no fabulous items that are too clichéd or uncool for you not to EMBRACE them …. There is no reason to listen to wind chime naysayers…. There is no concept out there so sacred that it isn't worth giving a TWIST to…. There is no family portrait so precious that it wouldn't look better with a mustache…. There is no fascinating place or character or idea in this world that you should not be open to EXPLORE…. There is no reason not to delve deeply into your subversive side…. There is no right or wrong way to live, just new ways of life to PONDER…. And there is no reason not to give yourself a break.

Creating the haimish home

There's nothing more depressing than a china cabinet, a dusty repository for things you ostensibly love but never want to touch. You should want to sit in every chair and to experience every thing—the people, the books, even the coasters—in your life. Often.

Simon and I built our dream home on Shelter Island with this very ethos in mind. The essence of Happy Chic dwelling is that informality and comfort will set you free. Always start with a chic and classique foundation—but then add ***a dash of humor, a pinch of quirk, a soupçon of folly.***

Family and friends are more important than objects. But those objects, and how you deal with them, can provide the setting in which to kibitz, dine, and decompress with your *haimisher menschen*—Yiddish for the people you feel (insanely) comfortable with. You should never want the meal, the conversation, or the fun to end.

Diaphanous beaded curtains delineate space and create intimacy without being too blocky. My favorite use of them is in the bar at the Four Seasons Restaurant in NYC (the AC even gives them subtle movement).

IT ALL STARTS WITH A CONVERSATION PIT

Conversation pits are one of the great legacies of modernism. I'm not the *feng-shui-iest*, but these spaces have an energy—a siren call—that draws you in for a moment of relaxed fun: the *sine qua non* of good design.

Low is lounge-y. We built a sofa into the wide step down to our living room so that it hovers over the area rug.

MAKE AN ENTRANCE

N° **02**

Doorknobs matter. When guests arrive at your abode, the doorknob is likely the first thing they'll touch, and the things one touches should have meaning. Make every one count.

We lacquered our door orange (meow!) and found a vintage knob and plate on eBay for a ***Brutalist chic touch.***

HAVE BREAKFAST IN A HAPPY PLACE

Cozy counts. Behold the power of a nook—the perfect yang to the conversation pit's yin. (Or is it the other way around?) Intimate and embracing, it's where you go to have some "me" time. Situate yours alfresco if you can, or in a room with a view. Grab the paper, gather fortifying foods, and take a moment to get your morning bearings.

SPOIL YOURSELF ROTTEN

N° **04**

Sometimes, it can feel like bad things happen only to you. As a preemptive move, bank happiness along the way by continuously spoiling yourself. *Spoilage need not be reserved for "special occasions"*; make it a point to do at least one of these things every day**.**

06
HAVE AN AFTERNOON TEA MOMENT

Those Brits know what they're doing. The 3 p.m. cuppa is simultaneously relaxing and pick-me-upping: the perfect pause. It's extra special if you have a vintage, floral, granny-licious pot. *And cookies.*

05
NAP IN ODD PLACES

My poor colleagues are constantly stumbling upon yours truly snoozing away in an improbable nook.

07
WATCH BAD TV

Reality shows like ***Real Housewives (of anywhere)*** numb life's troubles—and remind you just how good you have it.

08
COLLECT THINGS YOU LOVE

Gathering like with like, albeit in different sizes, shapes, and iterations, can be highly validating. Follow the same advice regarding foods and friends.

09
PUT DIANA VREELAND'S "WHY DON'T YOU?"'S INTO PLAY

Ideas in Diana Vreeland's *Harper's Bazaar* "Why Don't You?" column, which debuted in 1937, include tying black tulle bows on your wrists, having a yellow satin bed quilted in butterfly patterns, and remembering how delicious champagne cocktails are after tennis or golf. ***Well, why don't you?***

STACK TOWELS ON A BATHROOM CHAIR

N° 10

Instead of hiding them in a hall closet, keep a side order of thirsty towels stacked, spa-style, on four-legged perches. (It's a way to add lots of luxury to life without buying a single thing.)

GET TO KNOW

Henny Garfunkel

Environmental portraitist (a/k/a street photographer) Garfunkel captures the weird and the wonderful for everyone from *Vogue* to the NFL. Two toilets in the same bathroom? You never see that!

Same rules as an orgy: You need at least three as a minimum, then add on as many as you desire.

MAXIMALIZE THE BATH-ROOM

Treat it as a real room, not just a sanitary space. Add table lamps, art you love, and . . . why not retrofit a piece of furniture as your vanity?

One sink for a couple leaves more room for zhooshing.

BUILD AN OUTDOOR SHOWER

An al fresco shower lends beach-house chic to any home, even if it's far from the sea. Install a window to frame the view, be it surf or woods or suburban sprawl. Ours has the proportions of a wide-screen TV, so *it's like you're always watching* Swept Away.

TREE SHOWER

A tree shower (with thatch doors) like the one from *South Pacific* will help you wash that man right outta your hair.

WATERFALL

Before shower heads, there was the waterfall. Over a lagoon, it's a bathtub, too.

TWIG BOX

I fashioned this foxy box from twigs gathered from the yard—a rare *Gilligan's Island* homage that's both Ginger and Mary Ann.

INDUSTRIAL PIPING

This industrial-grade metal pipe is rustic and simple, without any enclosure.

CADILLAC DIY

Pimp your ride with extra amenities. This vintage Cadillac is equipped for a post–beach-day rinse.

N° **13**

PUSH THE LIMITS OF SCALE

Put a unique spin on the familiar by blowing it up. New York artist Andy Harman sat on the floor of his atelier and twisted the thickest natural jute cords he could find into shape, reinventing the macramé owl—a staple of the '70s—for my parlor. ***It takes five people to move!***

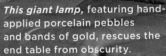

This giant lamp, featuring hand-applied porcelain pebbles and bands of gold, rescues the end table from obscurity.

Happy Chic Activity

MAKE YOUR OWN DECORATIVE OBJET D'ART

Idle hands and all. Nurturing your inner crafter develops new skill sets and a sense of accomplishment. Plus, it's supremely fun. Twisting your own wall-sized owl would be an unwise first stab, but you can work your way up by starting with this more diminutive hooter. Once finished, hang your masterwork on the wall for all to admire.

Welcome to Feral Hall—my humble Shelter Island abode.

DARE TO BE LEGENDARY

These digs push the envelope for excess, extravagance . . . and simplicity. As a bonus, they all have impressive names. Bestow a moniker on your domicile to give the impression that it's been in the family for decades, *even if you moved in last week.*

THE GROVE

One of my major design muses, **David Hicks**, built this fabulous folly in Oxfordshire, England. Its grounds are filled with avenues, vistas, and cozy outdoor rooms, galore.

DAWNRIDGE

The artist and designer **Tony Duquette** built this diminutive Beverly Hills palace of glam and glitz in 1949. Excess in the best way.

AYALA DE CHINATI

Outside of Marfa, Texas, comfortable ranches built by contemporary artist **Donald Judd** mix über-clean and Mexican-style pieces.

THE CABANON

Eccentric architect **Le Corbusier**'s 150-square-foot Côte d'Azur beach house is made from halved trees and plywood. Everything is built-in, like a ship's cabin on land.

SHANGRI LA

Heiress and philanthropist **Doris Duke** used this architectural gem in Honolulu, Hawaii, to house her enormous Islamic art collection.

No. 16

·HAPPY·CHIC·HERO·

AUNTIE MAME

One of my favorite rooms was never a room at all. Rather, it was a film set: the living area of Beekman Place in the 1958 classic, *Auntie Mame*.

TOPS THE BEST-SELLER! TOPS THE PLAY! THE ONE AND ONLY

They're all here! That mad marvelous 'Auntie Mame' mob!

Vera! The Duchess from Pittsburgh! Babcock! The Heckling Banker! Burnside! The Pride of Dixie! O'Bannion! The Hairy Lover! The Gruesome Miss Gooch!

"AUNTIE MAME"

STARRING

ROSALIND RUSSELL

FILMED IN TECHNIRAMA · COLOR BY TECHNICOLOR · PRESENTED BY WARNER BROS.

17 HAVE MULTIPLE SEATING ZONES

Carve out a few intimate zones within the larger whole, punctuating with lots of cocktail tables. (Caveat: Ultra-mod furniture can sometimes be antithetical to real life . . . and painful. *Get a comfy couch.*)

18 SEPARATE WITH SCREENS

They delineate space and add instant architecture. Perforated patterns are ideal when dividing areas. Solid screens are great in a corner.

19 REDECORATE OFTEN

Over the course of the movie, Mame recreates the space six times, evoking everything *from high Bollywood to Postmodern Neoclassical,* while embracing a bit of subversion along the way.

20 ROCK A HOSTESS FROCK

When entertaining (or even when it's Tuesday), don something splashier than your norm—*preferably floor-length and shimmery.*

LEARN TO SPEAK SCANDINAVIAN

Laplander Chic is an unheralded design idiom. Throw a sheepskin insouciantly over chairs for casual squish. You can buy them at IKEA for practically nothing.

PORCE-LAIN POWER

The all-white tableau is one of life's happy contradictions. Used judiciously, ***desaturation is a potent force***. (Caveat, decorator: Too much monochromatic madness can be a washout.)

My Charade collection uses improbable inspirations: Austrian poof drapes, wall mouldings, and equestrian studs.

DWELL

HAPPY

SURROUND YOURSELF WITH HAPPY AND YOU'LL BE HAPPY. SOUNDS SIMPLE, RIGHT? BUT IT'S TRUE. START WITH MY LISTS OF DWELL-CENTRIC TALISMANS TO FIND OUT WHAT MAKES YOUR TICKER TICK.

DWELL TUNES

MUSIC FOR DINNER AND COCKTAIL PARTIES

FLAUNT YOUR INTERNATIONAL SAVOIR-FAIRE WITH SOME LATIN FLAVOR

1. SÉRGIO MENDES' FAVORITE THINGS (1968)
   SÉRGIO MENDES

2. EL BAILE ALEMÁN (2000)
   SEÑOR COCONUT: Kraftwerk goes Cha Cha!

3. BEACH SAMBA (1966)
   ASTRUD GILBERTO

4. ER TWO (2010) LAS SEVENTIES: crowd pleaser

5. BLAME IT ON THE BOSSA NOVA (1963) EYDIE GORMÉ

DWELL MOVIES

GREAT INTERIORS ON CELLULOID

I. THE BOYS IN THE BAND (1970)
   groovy gays in Sutton Place

II. PILLOW TALK (1959)

III. THE PARTY (1968)
   The comical side of Modernism

IV. NORTH BY NORTHWEST (1959)

V. A SINGLE MAN (2009)
   swanky

DWELL BOOKS

1. ALEXANDER GIRARD BY TODD OLDHAM AND KEIRA COFFEE
   Best. Book. Ever.

2. AN ARCHITECTURE OF JOY BY MORRIS LAPIDUS

3. SLIM AARONS: LA DOLCE VITA

4. CALIFORNIA DESIGN, 1930-1965 BY WENDY KAPLAN

5. VERNER PANTON: THE COLLECTED WORKS
   Pop God!

DWELL GEAR

Things you should never live without

1. LEE PRESS-ON NAILS
   Make your guests wear them to spice up a dinner party.

2. 25-WATT BULBS
   Dim is glam.

3. MANISCHEWITZ
   Wine snobbism is sooo yesterday.

4. LL BEAN CAMOUFLAGE TOTE BAGS You can never have enough.

5. PING PONG TABLES
   Fun!

Love what you love

A famous(ish) magazine editor-in-chief once put me down for rollerblading. My response? I skated home and never gave it another thought. And a snooty socialite once told me that having a Japanese maple in my garden was "suburban." So I got two more. *Life's too short to cut yourself off from the things (and people) you're cuckoo for* just because someone else doesn't like them. Never start a sentence with "I'm (not) the type of person who . . ." Don't impoverish your life that way! Instead, embrace your inner blading, aerobics-loving, fad-following self. *Remember: Those who rejected disco missed out on the party.* Be sure to be the first to arrive and the last to leave.

24

GIVE SMALL SPACES SOME LOVE

Take advantage of a nook, an area between windows, or awkward corner, and transform it into an office. Find a narrow-profile desk that folds up or has built-in storage to whisk away papers when not in use. Borrow a chair or stool that tucks under the desk. *Don't skimp on good lighting or pleasing decorative bits.*

BLACK . . . MEET ORANGE

And not just on Halloween. This pairing of earthy tones is bold but never garish—and totally gorgeous. For the ultimate union, make sure one plays the lead and the other, a supporting role.

Abstraction, in the same palette, clarifies and supports.

PAOLO SOLERI

My wind chimes are by Paolo Soleri, an Italian visionary, utopianist, and designer. Originally from Turin, Italy, he opened a giant ceramics factory, on the Amalfi Coast, part of which became his atelier. He later settled in Scottsdale, Arizona, and formed the Cosanti Foundation, dedicated to experimentation in urban planning. Arcosanti is his fantastical prototype town and community in the middle of the desert. Begun in 1970, it feels like a hippy-dippy commune meets *Logan's Run*. **Visit it!**

The southern exposure of Soleri's ceramic windbells foundry at Cosanti (above) maximizes the warmth of the winter sun.

LOVE WIND CHIMES

I'm in heaven at dusk, when I sit on my deck, watch the ospreys hunt, and listen to the tinkly goodness of my wind chimes.

This bronze Soleri windbell makes beautiful music as its verdigris planes collide.

ADOPT A SIGNATURE FOLLY

Think of it as branding for the self. It can be sartorial, lifestyle ("Remember, Jean-Raphael simply refuses to eat yellow food . . ."), or anything that sets you apart from *hoi polloi*.

Anna Wintour's bob

Nicki Minaj's colorful wigs

my white pants

Simon Doonan's Liberty shirts

Karl Lagerfeld's Japanese fan

Anne Slater's blue lenses

Thurston Howell's foulard

SHALL WE DANSK?

If you're willing to sleep in a hotel bed, you're comfortable using things others have used before you. Among my most prized flea market finds are vintage Dansk pots and pans—*a whole lot groovier than a matched 10-piece set of All-Clad.*

I archive my pottery on a plywood shelf that runs the entire length of my kitchen.

Nº

30

GRANNY'S DANGLER

My grandmother spotted this gem outside an ironmonger's shop in Mexico, and it's one of my favorite things. The shapes and colors have always been an inspiration in my pottery.

My inspiration for this mug was Lady Bunny, who deserves a gold medal for hair—she never met a coif too high or too extravagant.

31
EXPERIMENT WITH HAIRSTYLES

Try on different hats, as it were, with a minimum of fuss (that is, until you start with new cuts and colors weekly, à la Linda Evangelista in the '90s).

The handle is a ponytail, too!

WISTERIA PERM

Dame Edna

WINGED "FARRAH"

Farrah Fawcett

MAXI FRO

Angela Davis

SEXY SHAG

Jane Fonda in *Klute*

TEASED-UP BUMP

Snooki

GIANT BOUFFANT

Lady Bunny

GAMINE PIXIE

Mia Farrow in *Rosemary's Baby*

N° 32

GET FELT UP

This definition-bender (part fabric, part art) is made by, yes, boiling woven wool fabric, which renders it ***very dense, soft, and delicious***. It takes color in an intense way—especially bright jewel tones like these. The felt pads that surround my floating fireplace provide comfort, a nice perch, and some visual punctuation.

GET TO KNOW

Joseph Beuys

Post-WWII German sculptor, performance and installation artist, professor, and shaman, Beuys is especially famous for his works in animal fat and felt.

PATINA IS PRICELESS

Sometimes a little wear and tear is good. (I've been described as waterfront property with a bit of hurricane damage.) These French Industrial lamps proudly display their war wounds. *Choose friends with a few dings, too.*

TAPESTRY DESERVES ITS DUE

Wall hangings like this deliver a welcome dose of sweetness—the antidote to a surfeit of "cool" in decorating. ***I say sweet is cool.*** And sophisticated examples bring it in a whole new way.

GET TO KNOW

Evelyn Ackerman

The hanging at my house is by Los Angeles–based artist Evelyn Ackerman, whose ceramics, mosaics, wood carvings, and tapestries lie in the place between mod and precious and exude the colors of her native California.

The undulating rims of
these bowls give them
a kinetic property.

35

USE
BOWLS AS
PLANTERS

Less predictable than terra cotta, these Wiggle
bowls are the perfect, unexpected place to grow
succulents. (My favorite category of plant, too—low
maintenance and hard to kill).

36

MAKE YOUR OWN VALENTINES

Embrace yourself as you embrace others. Putting pen, paint, ink and/or scissors to paper and making your own cards is a labor of love . . . and a total pain in the butt. That's why people appreciate it so much, especially on that prickliest of holidays, Valentine's Day. Spread the love with a little homemade craft, and *don't forget to make one for yourself.*

Happy Chic Activity

EMBRACE HUMBLE MATERIALS

Sometimes the least expensive solution is the best. Burlap is beautiful—underappreciated and cheap, too. In our bedroom, we used it for the drapes, which provide privacy but also let the sun shine in.

CORRUGATED ALUMINUM
MAKES YOUR ROOFTOPS
INDUSTRIALLY CHIC.

MASONITE FLOORS LOOK
BETTER, THE MORE
F*#KED UP THEY GET.

PEGBOARD CAST AS
SLIDING CABINET DOORS
IS SUBTLY GRAPHIC.

AFTER DE-NAILING AND
SANDING, THESE SCAFFOLDS
ARE SALVAGE SWANK.

GET HORNY

Genuine boney protrusions are rare, politically incorrect, and just a bad idea. So go faux with devilicious lamps that say you're naughty . . . but highly tasteful. *Give the devil his due—he's the original Bad Ass*.

HAVE A WOODLAND MOMENT

Our forest friends are having a well-deserved comeback. Create a folkloric tableau. I used a vintage driftwood lamp, ceramic fox, and nifty Blenko glass mushrooms for some *cheerful style à la Brothers Grimm*.

embrace HAPPY

THINKING TOO HARD CAN GET IN THE WAY OF GETTING YOUR HAPPY ON. OUR LISTS OF MUST-GIVE-INTO'S WILL UP YOUR ENJOYMENT FACTOR WITHOUT TAXING YOUR GREY MATTER IN THE LEAST.

NUMBER 1

EMBRACE TV SHOWS

CULTURALLY ILLITERATE? WATCH THESE SWEEPING DRAMAS FROM THE 80'S

THE THORN BIRDS (1983) Priest and parishioner fornicate; tragedy ensues.

FALCON CREST (1981) California winery as backdrop for Greek drama.

MAFIA PRINCESS (1996) Tony Curtis and Susan Lucci in one place.

FRESNO (1986) Serialized spoof of the genre featuring Carol Burnett.

NORTH AND SOUTH (1985) Swayze in a Mason-Dixon-straddling bodice ripper.

EMBRACE BOOKS

TRASHY

★ TRULY TRASHY NOVELS ★ THAT ARE UN-PUT-DOWN-ABLE

SCRUPLES BY JUDITH KRANTZ *Not trashy just great.*

THE HAPPY HOOKER BY XAVIERA HOLLANDER

ONCE IS NOT ENOUGH BY JACQUELINE SUSANN

THE OTHER SIDE OF MIDNIGHT BY SIDNEY SHELDON

HOLLYWOOD WIVES BY JACKIE COLLINS: *Delicious.*

EMBRACE GEAR

DON'T FEAR FASHION STATEMENTS...

1 **CAPES** Pink bullfighter, tweed Miss Marple, Picasso capes, capes, capes!

TWO **SENSATIONAL EYEWEAR** Think Iris Apfel, Peggy Guggenheim, Michelle Harper

III **FANS** Karl Lagerfeld stopped using one, so why don't you start?

GLITTER Belongs everywhere especially on your eyes and décolletage

5 **BOOM BOXES** Share your anthems with everyone within a mile range.

EMBRACE tunes

cozy up to country

"TICKS" (2007) BRAD PAISLEY
Country Lyrics rule. Period!

"JOLENE" (1973) DOLLY PARTON
Heartbreaking.

"AMARILLO BY MORNING" (1982) GEORGE STRAIT: Smooth George...

"RING OF FIRE" (1963) JOHNNY CASH
There's a reason it's a classic.

"KEROSENE" (2004) MIRANDA LAMBERT
Country riot gurrrrrl

Shake up your gray matter

Harmony has its place, but what really excites me is a bit of discord—a note or two out of balance, an element not quite "correct." It's a revelation, *like some Stravinsky after an overdose of Abba.*

I'm certainly an advocate for familiarity and comfort, but let's face it: predictability can be palliative. Your personal narrative just needs a few plot twists, some minor character adjustments, or perhaps a surprise ending. Some long-lasting adjustments take but a minute to execute; at the other extreme, you might want to try out a whole new personality.

If you've been seeing the world through rose-colored glasses, it's time to try blue for a change. Who knows—you might discover a new, better reality lurking beneath the surface. *Let's get twisted, sister!*

CUST-OMIZE WITH MURALS

Why should walls hold all the intrigue? Any place is a great place to have art in your life—the less expected, the more captivating. Murals are a surefire way to personalize and embellish some of the lesser surfaces around the house.

GET TO KNOW

John-Paul Philippe

Our pelican frieze is by extraordinaire NY-based architect/designer/artist/painter John-Paul Philippe. We asked him to create a mural inspired by views from our Shelter Island kitchen.

Outlier artist *Alexis Yeskey* made this phenomenal mirror frame from an array of balusters.

N° 4²

MAKE ART OUT OF THE UNEXPECTED

Oil on canvas is so three centuries ago. Art created from unusual materials exposes their hidden beauty. Found objects and reclaimed wood, for instance, can be the foundations for a modern masterpiece.

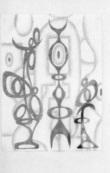

Malcolm Hill's painting harmonizes with the scrolly backs of the chairs.

43

USE CHAIRS AS SCULPTURE

Blur the line between furniture and art. You can always find some weird chair, maybe one that's teetery or uncomfortable, and plop it in a place you don't sit. *Voilà, an instant installation.*

Chuck D: vegetarian rapper, actor, activist, founder of Public Enemy; turns ugly noises into powerful sound.

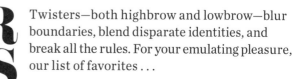

David Bowie: the original androgynous glam rocker, gender bender extraordinaire, and husband of goddess Iman.

Yoko Ono: diminutive Beatles breaker-upper (alleged), later avant-garde artist, singer, and peacenik.

Nº **44**

EMULATE OUR TWISTERS

Twisters—both highbrow and lowbrow—blur boundaries, blend disparate identities, and break all the rules. For your emulating pleasure, our list of favorites . . .

Quentin Crisp: British writer, storyteller, and gay icon, known for his extreme effeminacy and bitchiness.

RuPaul: the world's first drag queen supermodel, part-time singer-songwriter, and reality TV host.

Jeff Koons: American artist/sculptor; makes gigantic, stainless steel reproductions of balloon animals and other kitsch.

The artist formerly (and currently) known as Prince: high-heeled boot-wearing genre blender.

REUSE

AND
REPURPOSE

Using objects for other than their intended purpose brings untapped beauty to the fore, *like a nerdy girl who sheds her glasses and discovers mascara.*

Swap in these nautical brass cleats for everyday drawer pulls and . . . *Hello, sailor!*

NAUTIQUE MYSTIQUE

N°
46

A seafaring theme creates waves of happiness with a splash of whimsy. I paired a favorite C. Jeré brass boat with a rope-frame mirror and a trio of my Utopia mermaid and sailor vases. *Ahoy, chicness!*

47

PLAY YOUR ALTER EGO

Are you a bad seed? Try being a choir boy for a week. Prim and proper? ***Give the devil-may-care approach a spin.*** Saints and sinners alike will find liberation in acting out their opposites. You might never go back to your old ways.

N° 48 FLAME OUT

You don't have to be gay to enjoy this flamboyant meeting of color and pattern. My Bargello pillow is based on examples found in a palace in Florence. Their geometric undulations are the perfect foil for a solid divan or love seat.

N° 49

RECONSIDER THE SUITE OF FURNITURE

Identically styled sets got a bad rap during the game-show years, when ugly incarnations were handed out on *Let's Make a Deal.* When properly imagined and elegantly realized, though, the matching suite can have a calming effect. Its programmatic aspect is prim but needn't be proper.

A single orange piece breaks the matchy mold.

The Mies van der Rohe Barcelona series (1929)

The William Platner series (1966)

The Eero Saarinen Tulip series (1956)

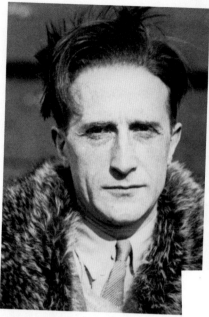

MARCEL DUCHAMP/ MONA LISA

Dadaist/Surrealist artist Marcel Duchamp added a mustache to his take on the world's most famous painting—and an inscription that sounds like "She has a hot ass" in French. *Vive la différence!*

L.H.O.O.Q.

51 BE IRREVERENT

Ever grow weary of being respectful and serious all the time? Of the sacredness of "fine art" and "important architecture"? I say it's O.K. to put down Titian or express annoyance at Palladio. (Just don't build a glass house . . .)

My bloke, Simon, brilliantly defaced this vintage GW print by adding an eyepatch, Dali-stache, and red lips. But the *pièce de résistance* was the Prince pendant.

52

DEFACE IT

Taking Sharpies or spray paint to other people's artwork is disrespectful, and a little destructive—in other words, more fun than you can imagine.

These Warren Platner chairs
never even saw it coming.

No 53

SWAP IT OUT

Think of it as a key party for your furniture. It's a small
move, but with high impact. Switch coordinating cushions
with one another, creating a look that's less rigid but still
supremely chic. Your neighbors will be scandalized!

MIX YOUR MESSAGES

N° 54

While I'm a major supporter of classical proportions and balance, I also love to mix stuff up. The best results often happen by plunking a couple of beloved objects on a table and seeing what happens.

55) SEE THE WORLD DIFFERENTLY

Is my purple The Purple Prince's yellow? Ever wonder what Paul Klee's take on downtown Scranton might look like? Our bipolar paint-by-numbers kit encourages you to ponder deep questions like these. Why paint in a naturalistic way when you can shuffle the hues? (I recommend choosing colors randomly for a real jolt in perspective.)

BLACK

The less fabulous something seems it would look painted all black, the more fabulous it will actually be. Houses, entire suites of furniture—even interior walls—*look smashing dressed head-to-toe in it.*

GET TO KNOW

Louise Nevelson & Arnold Scaasi

Sculptor Louise Nevelson once helped fashion designer Arnold Scaasi solve a decor dilemma by telling him to make everything black. (She famously practiced what she preached.) He did, and it was a revelation—he even ebonized his 80-year-old weekend cottage on Long Island.

57

AMP UP THE EVERYDAY

For this fancy bathroom I designed for the Kohler Design Center, I've crossed boundaries. Eclecticism is about more than just mixing: sometimes you have to take a theme and crank it to the limit. In this case, I haven't merely mixed old and new; I've crossed boundaries with a *2001*-inspired ***mash-up of Space Age, Hollywood Regency, and Mid-Century***—plus a few feathers for good measure.

TURN THIS ROOM INTO AN OUTFIT

One of my favorite mags ever (sigh) was *Domino*—brainchild of the incomparable Deborah Needleman—which seemed to magically embody much of my Happy Chic manifesto each month. In a particularly ingenious column called ***"Turn This Outfit Into A Room,"*** fashion was made to resemble home furnishings. I thought it would be fun to transform a happening room into a fetching ensemble.

BOHEMIAN MODERN (BOHO MOD)

YOUR MUSES
Jacqueline Bisset; Ali MacGraw; Sienna Miller; Talitha Getty; Marianne Faithfull; Charlotte Gainsbourg; Theda Bara

YOUR SOUNDTRACK
The Killers; Joss Stone; Fyrefly; Vampire Weekend; Buraka Som Sistema

YOUR HOLIDAYS
Glamping in Surrey; Hotel La Gazelle d'or, Morocco; Palm Springs; the 11ème

YOUR THREADS
Stella McCartney; Zandra Rhodes; DVF; Chloé; Top-Shop/Forever 21; Etsy

YOUR SNACKS
Annie's Cheddar Bunnies; Lärabars; champagne

Eccentric outsiders can be your shamans of it up; happiness. Shake it up; clash some culture; twist happy!

TWIST HAPPY!

TWIST MOVIES

TALES OF THE OUTCAST AND OUTLYING

1. **PARIS IS BURNING (1990)** Late 80s drag queens "voguing" away.
2. **THE MISFITS (1961)** John Huston/Arthur Miller tale of souls adrift in the West.
3. **EDGE OF SEVENTEEN (1998)** Eurythmics and Bronski Beat-laced coming-of-age story.
4. **PRETTY IN PINK (1986)** Wrong-side-of-the-tracks Molly Ringwald in this tale of moxie...and pinking shears.
5. **THE DOOM GENERATION (1995)** Post-apocalyptic L.A. twenty-somethings on the lam.

GEAR The stuff of instability

The stuff of instability

1. **THE BIGGEST PURSE YOU CAN FIND** To load with all manner of personal fetishes.
2. **FALSIES** Eyelashes, padded bras, press-on nails, codpieces
3. **PLATFORM SHOES** The greater the elevation, the greater the view.
4. **SUITS AND TIES (FOR WOMEN) COCKTAIL DRESSES (FOR MEN)** Give cross-dressing a whirl.
5. **CLASHING PRINTS** Bold, garish ones that don't coordinate at all. Wear them together.

Twist Tunes
psychedelic melodies to jangle your status quo

I RE (1990) LES RITA MITSOUKO

II DIG YOUR OWN HOLE (1997) THE CHEMICAL BROTHERS

III FOREVER CHANGES (1967) LOVE

IV SURREALISTIC PILLOW (1967) JEFFERSON AIRPLANE

V COQUELICOT ASLEEP IN THE POPPIES (2001) OF MONTREAL

TWIST BOOKS
PEOPLE WHO LEAD TWISTED LIVES

ONE FRUITS BY SHOICHI AOKI

TWO AMERICAN PSYCHO BY BRETT EASTON ELLIS: SICK BUT PROPHETIC

THREE FLOWERS IN THE ATTIC BY V.C. ANDREWS

FOUR FEAR AND LOATHING AT ROLLING STONE EDITED BY JANN WENNER

FIVE EXTREME BEAUTY IN VOGUE EDITED BY PHYLLIS POSNICK: THE SOFTER SIDE OF THE GROTESQUE

Swim in the pool of possibility

As you walk through the (well-tended) garden of life, keep your eyes wide open: *You never know where a perfect bloom or a tasty berry might be hiding.* It's time to stop with the "I don't have time to...," "I could never..." and "Someday I'll..." phrases that have been holding you back. Quit ogling that snapshot of rolling Napa Valley vineyards and buy a plane ticket. Stomp on some grapes and make some wine. Instead of keeping your photo collection on your computer, hang them on the walls and invite everyone you know over for an exhibition. The world, they say, is your oyster— *and I say it's time to start checking out all the varieties.*

MUSE #1: LIBERACE

MUSE #2: GARDINERS BAY

START FROM AN UNUSUAL PLACE

Having my pooch, Liberace, follow me around is like having an acolyte. For his devotion, I let him rest his weary self anywhere he wants—even on the good furniture. (He spends more time on it than we do.) We based the palette of our beach pad on *his naturally lustrous coat.*

ACCENT WITH AFRICANA

N° 61

Ancient civilization meets modernist trope. This Cameroonian Juju headdress delivers a loud note of feathered color over the master bed, but in a way that's so raffinée, graphic, and contemporary.

I made these tiles in a rich slate-gray glaze as a perfect contrast for the soft and bright headdress.

SUBVERT IT!

Probe the inappropriate parts of your mind, then go public with what you find. ***I couldn't NOT design a brass banana***—it lives proudly on a tiled coffee table at my house.

These hues draw from the adjacent pool and nearby vegetation.

SLAG IT OFF

Semitranslucent pressed "slag glass" was originally used to make decorative items in late 1800's England. You can pick up bags of it for a song and use it to *give texture and color to underappreciated areas*—indoors or out. I got the idea from Madame Ganna Walska (opposite) who lined the paths her garden, Lotusland, with it.

MADAME GANNA WALSKA

Born in Poland in 1887, Walska (née Hanna Puacz) was one of the first international *celebutantes* and the spiritual equivalent of Tony Duquette. She specialized in love, marrying six times while pursuing an opera career with great passion and, from most accounts, very little natural talent. Her final husband, a yoga specialist twenty years her junior, encouraged her to buy a large tract of land in California. When they divorced, Walska turned the property into a garden, collecting highly sought-after, rare, and exotic plants. Lotusland, as she called it, remains one of the best collections of flora in the world.

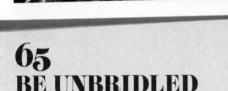

65
BE UNBRIDLED

Take a cue from Madame Walska: Don't be afraid to follow your dream and throw yourself into it full tilt—even if you're not any good at it.

67
ATTEND ADULT SUMMER CAMPS

Feel like a kid while finally (finally!) learning blacksmithing, glassblowing, pot-throwing or (no kidding) basketweaving at summer workshops offered by Haystack Mountain School of Crafts in Maine.

68
HAVE AN AIRSTREAM HOLIDAY

Wanderlust on wheels, American style: Everything you need is less than 15 feet away.

Nº
66

EXPLORE HAPPY CHIC DESTINATIONS

No need to sacrifice (life)style when you're on the road. These locales are lookers with personality to spare.

69
FIND AN OASIS

Preferably one that very chic aliens constructed in the middle of the desert. I reccomend the divine Amangiri resort near the Utah/Arizona border.

70
VISIT A DUDE RANCH

Latigo Dude Ranch in Colorado is an authentic place to get your Western on— with spectacular views, clean air, and, of course, *cowboys.*

♡ JADLER

71
STICK TO UNPRETENTIOUS SKI RESORTS . . .

. . . such as the Bromley Sun Lodge in Vermont. Often they're happier than the Euro-fabulous variety.

Welcome to Vermont

ST.TROPEZ

CAPRI

ACAPULCO

PAN AM

BERMUDA
IN 5 HOURS

PAN AMERICAN
AIRWAYS

IMPERIAL
AIRWAYS

DRINK IN LIFE'S JET-SET MOMENTS

While I extol the virtues of simple pleasures taken at home among close friends, there's a lot to be said for occasional globetrot. Ultra-swanky accommodations, "friends" you'll never see again, new sights and smells to animate the senses—***pass the Bain de Soleil.***

MONTE CARLO

HOP ON A GREY-HOUND BUS

N° 73

Some of my happiest moments were had when I was at my most destitute. Something about having so little means you also have less baggage (of all varieties). That's not to say the glamorous life ain't grand . . . but *Fresno makes Palm Springs possible.*

Midnight Cowboy—depressing and brilliant—plays out on a greyhound bus.

N° 74 GET GLITZY

No matter how large you're living, you can always use more shine and sparkle. Gold is yellow's happier-yet-bitchier cousin, and it seems to capture energy (and attitude) directly from the universe. Cover yourself, and your home, *in its Kardashian embrace.*

N° 75 SOAR WITH THE BIRDIES

Our chirping, feathered friends exude happiness. *(Think Snow White, not Alfred Hitchcock.)* Plus the unifying theme allows you to mix media (pillow, mobile, painting, ceramics) and lots of colors with aplomb.

GET TO KNOW

Higgins Glass

This studio was founded in Chicago in 1948, employing old techniques to create revolutionary, modern pieces. Today, the heirs continue to craft pieces such as this bird mobile.

LIVE LIKE ROYALTY

You are the ruler of your own domain, so you might as well get the most out of it. Think of your armchair as a jewel-encrusted throne; your bathrobe as an ermine-trimmed cape; your spatula, a scepter. To help you along coronation road, don our string art crown and start referring to yourself as "we."

BRING ON THE SUN AND THE SEA

Even if you live in Minnesota, you can rock a year-round beachy vibe in your home. Choose accessories with bright, saturated colors and metallic accents in crisp, graphic patterns.

These Santorini vases are as refreshing as a dip in the Aegean.

ESALEN INSTITUTE

Enrich your citified self at this 120-acre, hillside retreat center in Big Sur, California. The place was designed by architect Mickey Muennig, a local hero whose structures seem to grow out of the land.

79 SKINNY DIP WITH STRANGERS

Warning—or bonus—Esalen is clothing-optional.

80 TRANSFORM A PILE OF ROCKS INTO A TABLE

Fancy yourself a local artisan by stacking planes of slate, granite, or shale to make outdoor furniture. It's Brutalist meets Primitivist—*or Frank Lloyd Wright after a fistfight.*

HAVE A SLIM AARONS MOMENT

One of my fave photographers, Aarons is a ***documenteur par excellence*** of celebs and socialites. He was particularly fascinated by swimming pools and those lounging around them. Try channeling a jet-set vibe next time you and a Lionel Shriver novel are headed poolside.

82

BEHOLD THE OUT-DOOR LIVING ROOM

It's a study in contrasts—exposed yet protected, formal yet casual. To optimize its effects, offer lots of seating options, including a comfy couch and a couple of slouchy chairs. As long as it's all waterproof, the sky's the limit.

EXPLORE

MOVIES

INSTEAD OF REACHING FOR YOUR FAVORITE MAGAZINE OR LISTENING TO THE SAME OLD TUNES, GET OUTSIDE YOUR COMFORT BUBBLE AND EXPAND YOUR HORIZONS

TITLES FOR SOME EASY ESCAPISM

I. LET'S GET LOST (1988) Moody tribute to Chet Baker.

II. LOST HORIZON (1937) Westerners stranded in Shangri-la.

III. THE LOST BOYS (1987) California biker/vampires.

IV. LOST IN TRANSLATION (2003) Existential ennui in Tokyo.

V. LOST IN SPACE (1960's TV SERIES) Space colony family vs. gay stowaway.

EXPLORE BOOKS

LIFE GUIDES FOR THE ARMCHAIR TRAVELER

1 ON THE ORIGIN OF SPECIES BY CHARLES DARWIN

2 THE RAZOR'S EDGE BY W. SOMERSET MAUGHAM

3 TRAVELS IN WEST AFRICA BY MARY H. KINGSLEY A true pioneer in crinolines.

4 TRASHYTRAVEL.COM So wrong, it's right

5 THE SHOW GIRL NEXT DOOR: HOLLY MADISON'S LAS VEGAS

EXPLORE GEAR....

HAPPY CHIC **CARRY ONS**

01 DRAMAMINE, AMBIEN, EXCEDRIN PM Whatever it takes

02 FREAKY FACEMASK Leave me alone!

03 YOUR PET The ultimate attention-getter. Sooooo cute!

04 PARTY FAVORS Instant onboard community.

05 DRY SHAMPOO for a quick tress refresher

EXPLORE TUNES

FOREIGN SOUNDTRACK ARTISTS AND THEIR FAMOUS FILMS

1 NINO ROTA AMARCORD (1973), THE GODFATHER (1972).

2 FRANCIS LAI UN HOMME ET UNE FEMME (1966), LOVE STORY (1970)

3 MICHEL LEGRAND THE UMBRELLAS OF CHERBOURG (1964), THE THOMAS CROWN AFFAIR (1968).

4 RYUICHI SAKAMOTO THE LAST EMPEROR (1987), THE SHELTERING SKY (1990).

5 ENNIO MORRICONE THE GOOD, THE BAD & THE UGLY (1966), ONCE UPON A TIME IN AMERICA (1984).

Take yourself off autopilot

A whole new approach to life is often staring you in the face, but habit causes you to pass it right by. As an antidote, ***I say it's high time to put into practice a few novel ways of thinking*** and watch the world transform itself as if by magic! This chapter contains a series of clever ideas you might not think of in the course of a typical day—everything from how to make your bedroom a stage or use gravel to zhoosh-up your garden to the core philosophies of some of my favorite thinkers. In the end, ***it's about taking a look at the normal, the predictable, and the ho-hum that has come to define "you"*** and considering how you might change it up—for the better.

GRAVEL IS GOOD

N° 84

Large areas carpeted with small stones is part Buddhist monastery, part Parisian sculpture garden—think of it as *Zen Français*. Very small pebbles are more akin to sand, while coarser rocks (my preference) are more textural and produce a satisfying crunch underfoot.

Gravel is impossible to navigate in heels, so women (and drag queens) need to remove their Louboutins before crossing.

Dry Zen garden at Reiun-in Temple, Kyoto, Japan

Château de Villandry, Indre-et-Loire, France

Château de Drée, Burgundy, France

PONDER PERFORATION

N° 85

"*Delicate*" and "*industrial*" aren't terms you often hear applied to one object, but there's an appealing lightness to decorative items made from powder-coated perforated metal. This very stylish bathroom mirror is by Mathieu Matégot.

Placing a mirror opposite brightly colored walls gives the room an unexpected cheerful pop.

GET TO KNOW

Mathieu Matégot

This Hungarian/French master of steel tubing and punched-out sheet metal reached his artistic apex in the 1950s, creating limited editions of 200 of each piece. Famous pieces include the Copacabana and Nagasaki chairs—both of which incorporate his signature perforation.

This piece puts a new spin on the classic GW bust by mixing 2D, 3D, classicism, and craft. His silhouette has been torqued and extruded . . . with gold accents.

IMAGINE A WORLD WHERE YOU'RE PRESIDENT

Okay, not of the U.S. of A., but of your own life. Contemplate your own greatness and what you could achieve with it. Set up a committee (or at least a really magisterial desk). Get dressed in a suit, even if you're not leaving home. And treat your family and friends as the loyal citizens you know they can be.

PUT TABLES UNDER TABLES

N° 87

One can never a have sufficient number of low tables and cubes at the ready. They provide easily accessible perches for dinner in front of the TV, cocktails and canapés, or a sudden pile up of the latest magazines. Stacking them fills spatial voids and saves on real estate when they're not in use.

HAMPTONS

JONATHAN ADLER

SLIM AARONS · ONCE UPON A TIME

Nº

88 THE GENIUS THAT IS THE ÉTAGÈRE

This simple framework creates a visual hierarchy in three tableaux. Place larger clusters at the base, a playful pairing in the center, and a single punctuation mark at the top. *It's like a bookshelf with something extra— and without the weight.*

ECHO OUR PONDERERS

There are a lot of philosophies and -isms out there that you can use as your guide to life. Or, like those below, you can trail-blaze a different view. I just love to ponder the way these people think, and I think you should, too.

Steve "Wheels of Zeus" Wozniak: Steve Jobs was a genius marketer, but we are Team Engineer!

Camille Paglia: not your typical dissident feminist bête noire intellectual cranky pants. Pro-Madonna and Pro-Barbra.

Fran Lebowitz: intellectual, humorist, and consummate New Yorker who penned, "The opposite of talking isn't listening. The opposite of talking is waiting."

Patrick Dennis: genius who dreamed up *Auntie Mame* and later became a butler named Tanner.

Mr. Mickey: *Paper Magazine's* editorial director and all-around beautiful-life commentator.

Patrick Dennis

Mickey Boardman

Kim Kardashian

Kim Kardashian: from sex tape to reality starlet/businesswoman, ponder the magic of an unexamined life.

90

FIND A WAY TO HANG IT

Art against tile, instead of a plain wall, works like a beautiful marriage: the two complement and elevate one another. ***Plus, it's just a tad excessive.*** Remember: Gladys Knight was far greater with the Pips.

This painting on the tile
wall is actually hung via
chains from the ceiling.

The path outside our beach house consists of cast concrete stepping-stones on a bed of crushed seashells. We collected orange and yellow shells for an Andy Goldsworthy touch.

N°
91 ART IT UP!

Make ye art where ye may. Environmental installations turn a pile of leaves into sculpture, pinecones into a painting. You can even go indoors, arranging polished rocks into a zen garden swirl on your living room floor.

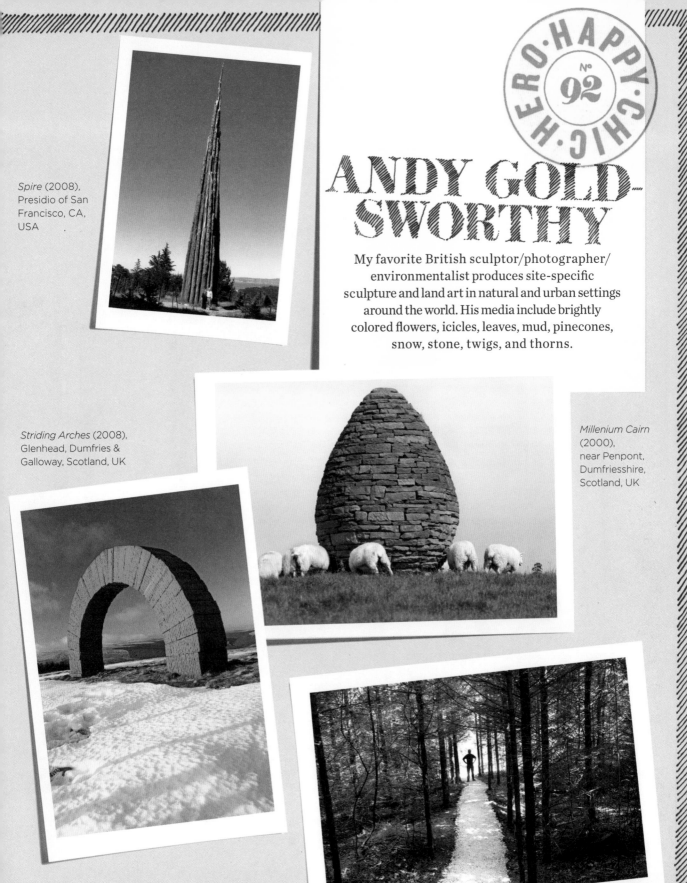

ANDY GOLD-SWORTHY

My favorite British sculptor/photographer/ environmentalist produces site-specific sculpture and land art in natural and urban settings around the world. His media include brightly colored flowers, icicles, leaves, mud, pinecones, snow, stone, twigs, and thorns.

Spire (2008), Presidio of San Francisco, CA, USA

Striding Arches (2008), Glenhead, Dumfries & Galloway, Scotland, UK

Millenium Cairn (2000), near Penpont, Dumfriesshire, Scotland, UK

Moonlit Path (2002), Petworth Park, West Sussex, England, UK

N° 93 RETHINK THE BOOKSHELF

Don't think of it as a mere repository; rather, keep your shelves vital and integrated. Here, we re-visioned the bookshelf as an architectural focal point of grand scale, mixing heavy plank and humble pegboard. Incorporate *objets*, art, and other un-bookish things to **turn a storage unit into a composition.**

PUNCTUATE WITH POPS
OF COLOR

CREATE A HIPPIE-DIPPIE
LOVE MOMENT

SAY OUI TO THE
TABLEAU VIVANT

MOUNT PICTURES AT
THE SHELVES'
CROSSING POINTS.

CHIC SATANIQUE

94

SPACE OUT WITH CROSS-STITCH

While engaging in repetitive craftivity, the mind has room to wander. You might remember a song title you couldn't recall earlier in the day or a long-forgotten incident that cracks you up when you least expect it. *Get out your yarn basket and enjoy the trip!*

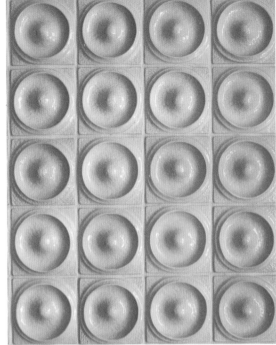

My inspiration for the tiles on this wall comes from Eva Hesse's iconic circle drawings, which soften rigorous modernism through warm craft—just what I aspire to do in my own work.

N°
95
PONDER
APRÈS

Enjoying some après-whatever means you've been doing something life-affirming and wondrous, and now it's time to kick back and appreciate yourself. But what if you just did that all the time? Après-ski is common, but *feel free to enjoy après-boiling water, après-turning on a light, etc.*

HANG CURTAINS BEHIND THE BED

Instead of a flat painted wall or fussy paper, place your bed(s) before floor-to-ceiling curtains to add backstage drama (plus depth and texture). *You might even get a standing ovation.*

TURN A CLOSET INTO A GUESTROOM

For an extra dose of drama, extend the curtains around the entire room to create a luxurious tent.

No 98
DON'T OVER-THINK IT

Part of living life to the fullest is not wasting hours spinning your wheels. Swat the little angel on your shoulder away and go with your gut instead.

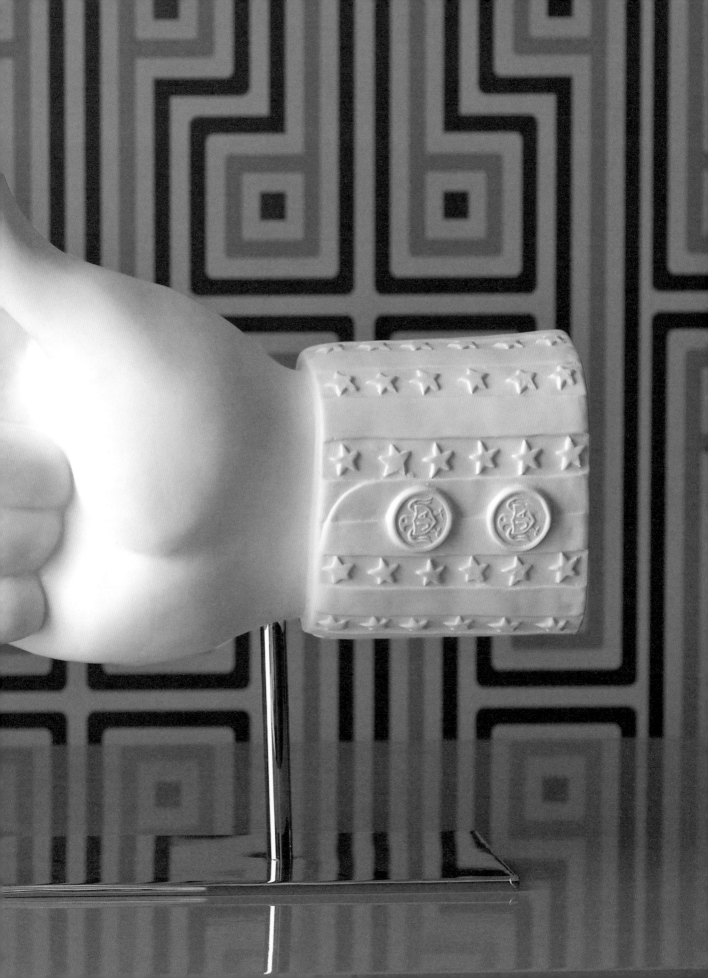

PONDER HAPPY

#99

crack open these tomes to teach you life's lessons as en Vogue sagely put it: Free your mind & the rest will follow

PONDER MOVIES

REMINDERS OF THE IMPORTANT THINGS IN LIFE

1. **I AM LOVE (2009)**
Even the most attractive family is bonkers.

2. **BARRY LYNDON (1975)**
Vanity ain't fair.

3. **IVAN THE TERRIBLE, PART I (1944)**
Even tsarinas get the blues.

4. **DANCER IN THE DARK (2000)**
How weird is Bjork?

5. **DEATH IN VENICE (1971)**
Don't go chasing rainbows!

PONDER SPORT

SOLO SPORTS FOR SOME NEW SELF-PERSPECTIVE

1. ROLLERBLADING
2. RIBBON DANCING
3. PADDLE BOARDING
4. ARCHERY
5. GYRO WHEEL

PONDER BOOKS

adopt a new philosophy

ONE IN DEFENSE OF FOOD BY MICHAEL POLLAN

TWO ECCENTRIC GLAMOUR BY SIMON DOONAN
Empowerment through beauty.

THREE ATLAS SHRUGGED BY AYN RAND
the pursuit of self-interest

FOUR ALICE'S ADVENTURES IN WONDERLAND BY LEWIS CARROLL
slip down the rabbit hole

FIVE ON THE ROAD BY JACK KEROUAC

PONDER TUNES

songs that bring up tough questions

① OLIVIA NEWTON-JOHN, "HAVE YOU NEVER BEEN MELLOW?" (Well, have you?)

② BEE GEES, "HOW CAN YOU MEND A BROKEN HEART?" (it ain't easy)

③ THE WHO, "WHO ARE YOU?"

④ JOE JACKSON, "IS SHE REALLY GOING OUT WITH HIM?"

⑤ CHARLENE, "I'VE NEVER BEEN TO ME" (has anyone, really?)

100

WHEN ALL ELSE FAILS... SAY IT WITH A PILLOW

Bold sentiments are difficult to profess—hence many a rock anthem. Let a chatty throw pillow bestow your fond feelings instead. It's a smooth move your paramour won't be expecting, or a way to express adoration for friends and family in a very public way. And it looks fabulous on the couch.

Love is the essence of Happy Chic!!!

MY HAPPY CHIC LIFESTYLE IS ENTIRELY DEPENDENT ON

the talented people I collaborate with and who helped make this book possible. Thank you to . . .

My Family: Amy, David, Harry, Mom, my late father, my Norwich terrier, Liberace, and my favorite person on Earth—my hubby, Simon.

JA Peeps: A thank you to the entire JA team, from the warehouse, the stores, the office, and the design studio.

And a special thanks to those who worked on the book: Ben Brougham and Liz Korutz.

Fearless Leaders: Gary Fuhrman, Erik Baker, and David Frankel.

The people who helped me build my dream house: Lisa Gray and Alan Organschi, Carlos Routh, Vicki Cardaro, John Paul Phillipe, Edwin Vera, and Leslie Degler.

Photographers: Joshua McHugh, Philip Ficks, and Mayo Studios.

Sterling Book Team: Pam Horn, Ashley Prine, Melanie Madden, designer Matthias Ernstberger, and illustrator Bruno Grizzo.

Deborah Needleman: You're the adorablest.

And to the threesome who slaved away to create this book: the fabulous Lisa Bubbers, my favorite chaperone, the divine Charlotte Hillman Warshaw, and most especially the witty and wise Stephen Treffinger.

ALL THE VOCABULARY YOU NEED TO SPEAK HAPPY CHIC!

après
A blissful state of being; that styling, relaxed glow you feel after doing something. Or nothing.

Bohemian Modern (Boho Mod)
A lifestyle choice I get way behind; slouchy chic with "free love" overtones. Think Marrakesh. Think ethnic textiles on a Dunbar sofa. Think Talitha Getty, the ultimate "Rich Hippie."

brass-tastic
A word used to celebrate the triumphant return of brass fixtures, furniture, and objets. *Brass is glamorous but warm at the same time. And don't even get me started on brass with a patina.* See **patina**

Brutalism
Reviled but gorgeous mid-twentieth century architectural style characterized by concrete bunkers and muscular shapes (clunky but ultra-chic). The late, great Paul Rudolph popularized it, and classicist Prince Charles hates it.

canapé
Tasty tidbit, or a decorative French antique sofa. *Either way, it's a winner.*

celebutante
One who is famous for being famous (e.g., Paris Hilton, Kim Kardashian). *Nice work if you can get it.*

cocktail table
Tussy word for "coffee table." *In other "flossy flossy" news, I've been told to always say* sofa *instead of* couch *and* curtains *instead of* drapes. See **tussy**

Coromandel screen
Long-forgotten decorating staple, these wooden folding screens are coated in dark lacquer, painted gold, and decorated with precious stones. *Coco Chanel collected them.*

craftastic
A word used to describe life-enhancing and décor-enhancing craft projects. *When facing a decorative dilemma, always consider a crafty solution, like wrapping a banister in rope or repainting a campaign-style chest. Get* craftastic.

décorotica
The use of sexy elements like animal prints and soft lighting to set the mood. *Provocative design is good design.*

drinks trolley
Essential lifestyle tool that brands you the "hostess with the mostest." *I don't drink, but I think* that drinks trolleys *should be everywhere.*

ecotante
Environmentally conscious debutante. (Formerly known as a Trustifarian.)

ermine trim
Usually an adornment on royal capes and crowns; an OTT touch when you need to kick up the glam up five notches. See **OTT**

étagère
Triangular-shaped shelving unit that narrows towards the top; the ultimate trophy case. *Nifty in improbable places, like a bedside table or entry foyer.*

flokati
Handmade wool shag rug of Greek origin. Before Moroccan Beni Ourain rugs became the "Rich Hippie" floor covering of choice, flokatis ruled. *They still look fab!*

folly
A costly, impractical, and ornamental building or practice—*in other words, nirvana!*

glunge
Glamour meets grunge; high meets low.

haimish
Adjectival form of "haimisher"; cozy, totally comfortable.

Hicksian
As in David Hicks, the king of mod geometrics mixed with traditionalia and bold colors. *Respect!*

inferior desecrator
Famous accusation made by Frank Lloyd Wright of Dorothy Draper that the design community has re-appropriated as a badge of honor. *(Architects notoriously hate decorators.)*

juju
Traditional West African object associated with witchcraft/religion. For *Modernist bona fides, I always like to add a dash of Africana.*

kibitz
Yiddish for chitchat—overlapping, loud, often unnecessary, and affectionate.

Laplander Chic
Use of cold-climate style (antlers, pelts, lingonberries) for stylish effect.

mantique:
Patinated object with a butch flavor (e.g., armor, pipes, brass valet stands). *Ralph Lauren is "King of the Mantique."*

maximalism
Opposite of minimalism; trick that pony out!

mishigas
Yiddish for "craziness," a state we should all strive for.

mothic
Mix of "mod" and "gothic." Think claw-foot chair reupholstered in an Alexander Girard stripe.

naff
British slang for nasty, in bad taste. See S. Doonan's *Gay Men Don't Get Fat* (best book ever) for explanation of *naff*.

nautique
Nautical, but everything sounds tussier in French. See **tussy**

Neo-Neoclassicism
Using Greek and Roman elements, but in a totally modern way. *Classicism is great, but one should always strive to make the familiar fresh.*

objet
Forget the English word "object"; *objet is much tussier.* See **tussy**

occasional table
Term for a small, often unanchored table that should be within easy reach, at all times. *You need more occasional tables than you might think.*

-ophile
Lover of, as in Francophile (all things French), retrophile (things from the past), or canophile (dogs). *Use liberally to add savoir faire.*

Organic Modernism
Design style characterized by sinuous lines inspired by nature. Think Eva Zeisel and Henning Koppel.

OTT
Over the top. Patron saints: Tony Duquette, Iris Apfel, and Louis XIV.

ornamental hermit
Ye olde English practice by wealthy eccentric estate owners of installing an aged bearded man on the grounds to delight and surprise guests. *The eighteenth-century tradition of housing a human pet at the bottom of your garden to impress the neighbors is set to return!*

patina
The surface beauty an object (or loved one) collects over time. *Everything gets better with age.*

Psychedelic Victoriana
That fabulous melding of Victorian ornament with trippy psychedelia that coalesced in San Francisco in the 1960s; scrolly, purple/black, mind-expanding design. *Anna Sui is keeping the dream alive.*

punim
Yiddish for "face," as in, "Oy, the punim on that one!" (used as a compliment . . . usually).

Reform Temple style
All of my favorite styles—Organic Modernism, Brutalism, OTT, with a top note of Womynian Craft—come together in the majesty of Reform Judaism temples. See **Organic Modernism, Brutalism, OTT, Womynian Craft**

salvage swank
Discards that you find and turn into something of beauty through repurposing.

-scape
Word ending appropriated into the design world by David Hicks, who famously called the arrangement of objects on a coffee table a "tablescape." *Other important "scape"-ortunities include* bedscape, sofascape, *and the ever-popular* manscape.

Skandi
Scandinavian; shorthand for clean, Nordic design.

Silverlake
Named for L. A.'s Brooklyn, a hipster mix of Mid-Century quirk and lots of plywood.

slubby
Irregularly textured weaves, usually due to variable thickness of natural yarn. *Always choose the* slubbiest *option*.

Steampunk
Industrial meets Old Curiosity Shoppe, meets bell-jar terrariums, with a heapin' helping of taxidermy.

tableau (pl: tableaux)
An artful grouping things to create a story or a "moment." See **-scape**

tussy
Fancy shmancy (syn. "flossy flossy"; see Fergie's hit "Glamorous"). Coined by Mayer Rus, Design & Culture Editor of the *Los Angeles Times Magazine*.

ungepatchke
Yiddish term for unnecessarily ornate or over-decorated.

Warholian
As in Andy Warhol; fast and pop and colorful and uptown and downtown and ironic and sincere (*a.k.a. what everything should be*).

Waspy Chic
Palm Beach country club style. Best seen through the work of the late, great Albert Hadley.

Womynian Craft
Feminist art and craft movement in which traditional female pursuits such as knitting and macramé are re-appropriated and subverted. Patroness saints: Judy Chicago, Sheila Hicks, Eva Hesse, Claire Zeisler, Georgia O'Keefe.

Zen Français
The love child of contemplative minimal and chic-at-birth. Think Christian Liaigre.

zhoosh (up)
To futz with; to fluff; to give a little love to; to freshen (usually décor).

PHOTO CREDITS

© Philip Ficks: 8, 12, 33, 36, 42, 61, 64, 73, 76, 90 (top left, bottom left), 131 (bottom left, top right)

© Christophe.Finot: 119 (bottom)

Ganna Walska Lotusland Foundation: 95 (center) © Bill Dewey

Getty Images: 11 (bottom right) © Ed Clark/Time & Life Pictures; 39 (bottom right) © Chaunce Hayden; 109 (top), Michael Ochs Archive; 39 (top center) © Terry O'Neill; 39 (center), Silver Screen Collection; 39 (bottom left), Theo Wargo/WireImage

© Estelle Hanania: 21 (bottom right)

Courtesy of Heritage Auctions: 22 (top), 39 (top right, bottom center)

Interior Archive: 21 (top left) © Fritz von der Schulenburg/TIA Digital Ltd

iStockphoto.com: 11 (center) © David Garry

© Judd Foundation. Licensed by VAGA, NYC. Courtesy of Judd Foundation Archives: 21 (center right)

Knoll, Inc.: 69 (top)

Courtesy of Kohler Co.: 83

Mayo Studios: 24–25, 52, 67–68, 108

© Joshua McHugh: pages x, 1–5, 9-10, 11 (top right), 13–15, 17, 19–20, 23, 28–31, 37, 40–41, 43–47, 50–51, 53, 56–60, 65–66, 69 (center, bottom), 71–72, 74–75, 82, 84, 88–89, 91–94, 100–103, 105–106, 110–113, 116–118, 120–121, 126–128, 130, 131 (top left, center, bottom right), 132–133, 135–136, 138–140

Newscom.com: 109 (center) © Sacramento Bee/ Lezlie Sterling

Shutterstock.com: 11 (bottom left) © AISPIX by Image Source; 119 (top, center) © Sergii Rudiuk

© Tim Street-Porter: 21 (top right)

SuperStock: 99

Jonathan Adler Crafts:

Designed by Patrice Boerens:
    Cross-stitch letter

Designed by Matthias Ernstberger:
    Paint-by-number

Designed by Cathi Milligan:
    Macramé owl

Designed by Kathleen McCafferty:
    LOVE linocut cards, String-art crown

INDEX

JONATHAN ADLER

The ultimate design hyphenate, Jonathan Adler is a TV personality, interior decorator, housewares entrepreneur, sharp-witted cultural authority, and mad potter. His empire now encompasses myriad product lines—from pillows and plates to furniture and lighting—sold in his twenty-two retail stores and hundreds of wholesale outlets. He is dedicated to bringing style, craft, joy, and a general feeling of grooviness to your home.